T0063638

Edgar Degas

*He saw the world
in moving moments*

Written by
Amy Guglielmo

Illustrated by
Skylar White

Hilaire-Germain-Edgar De Gas—or Edgar Degas, as we know him today—was born in Paris, France, in 1834. Edgar was the firstborn child in his family, but he would soon have two younger brothers, Achille and René, and two younger sisters, Thérèse and Marguerite.

Edgar grew up in a wealthy family. His grandfather started a bank in Italy and his father, Auguste, owned and ran the Paris office of the bank. Edgar's mother, Célestine, was from New Orleans, Louisiana, in the United States. Edgar loved to hear his mother's stories about her family in America.

In the 1800s, Paris was the art center of the world. On Sundays, when Edgar was a young boy, his father took him to music recitals, concerts, museums, and galleries. Edgar saw the works of great artists throughout history as well as drawings and paintings done by artists working in Paris at that time.

Though he spent his days banking, Edgar's father was also very interested in art. He had many friends who were artists, musicians, and art collectors. Edgar enjoyed his visits to family friends to see their art collections.

When he was eleven, Edgar entered the Lycée Louis-le-Grand, one of the top schools in France.

There, he studied Latin, Greek, ancient history, and music. He was a determined and dedicated student, but he often spent time doodling in class.

Try **doodling someone** in a **cartoon-like style.**

As an extra subject, Edgar took drawing lessons, which were his favorite. Compared to other students, Edgar's drawings didn't stand out, but his father noticed his artistic talents and encouraged him to continue his practice.

Tragically, when Edgar was thirteen, his mother died.
The Degas family was heartbroken, and his father never
remarried. Edgar missed his mother. He missed hearing
her stories about her family in America. Someday he
would go and see for himself.

After Edgar graduated from Louis-le-Grand, he entered law school because his father wanted him to take over the family business. But Edgar dreamed of being an artist, and instead of going to class he went to a famous art museum in Paris called the Louvre to see the artworks that filled the walls. Edgar also began to paint and draw in the museum, copying some of his favorite works.

When Edgar told his father he wanted to become an artist, his father was not happy. His father thought that being a banker was more practical, and he was worried about his son's future. Eventually, Edgar's father allowed him to study with an art teacher and even turned a room in the house into an artist's studio.

In 1855, Edgar entered the École des Beaux-Arts in Paris, one of the best art schools in the world. At school he learned about different styles of art, drew from models and sculptures, and kept copying at the Louvre.

One day while drawing, Edgar met his idol, artist Jean Auguste Dominique Ingres. Ingres was known for his disciplined style. He told Edgar, *"Draw lines, young man, draw lines."* After that, Edgar worked tirelessly at drawing.

Edgar soon grew frustrated with the classes at the École des Beaux-Arts, and felt that he could learn more studying on his own. Edgar decided to travel to Italy to discover the great Italian artists.

In Italy, Edgar was delighted by the scenery and inspired by the paintings he saw in museums and churches. Every day, Edgar worked hard to improve his skills. He learned how to make prints. He sketched and painted self-portraits, buildings, and landscapes, and copied famous paintings over and over again to get them just right.

Find a building that you think looks interesting. Draw it!

For three years, Edgar stayed with his father's family in both Naples and Florence. There, he learned to speak Italian and studied the historic art and architecture of Italy. Edgar enjoyed seeing his relatives, and he often asked them to pose for portraits because they were always available. And if they weren't around, he would just draw himself!

By the time he left Italy, he had recreated hundreds of works of art and filled many sketchbooks.

When Edgar returned to Paris, at age 25, his father gave him a large studio and an allowance. This meant that, unlike some other artists he knew, Edgar didn't need to sell his paintings to make a living. He could paint whatever he wanted! He excitedly began work on a painting that would become his first masterpiece, *The Bellelli Family*.

In *The Bellelli Family*, Edgar combined some of the sketches of his Italian relatives onto one giant canvas. The painting captures Edgar's aunt, uncle, and cousins looking in different directions to show that the family was unhappy and tense at that time. Edgar spent hours, days, months, and years reworking the painting.

In Paris, Edgar continued his studies and paid special
attention to the history paintings in the Louvre.
One day, while at the museum, he met Édouard Manet.
Manet was part of a group of artists who painted pictures
of modern life. Edgar and Manet became friends. Manet
encouraged Edgar to try new styles and subjects, like city
scenes and daily life.

Edgar would often make portraits of his artist friends.
One time Edgar painted a portrait of Manet and his wife
as a gift. Manet cut it up because he didn't like the way
Edgar had painted his wife. Edgar was so upset he took
the painting back!

In the 1860s, horse racing was a popular pastime in France. Edgar first started sketching horses on a visit to his childhood friend's house in Normandy in 1861. Later, in the 1870s, he went to Longchamp racetrack in Paris. Perhaps he was following Manet's advice to paint daily life or pursuing his interest in drawing and painting things that move. For hours on end, Edgar filled pages in his sketchbooks with focused jockeys, energetic horses, and fashionable spectators.

*Draw your favorite **animal**! What does it look like when it is **moving?***

Edgar captured the horses' movements with bold colors and dark shadows. Sharp diagonal lines drew attention to the horses' long, graceful limbs and strong muscles. Edgar rarely painted horses during the actual races.

Edgar sketched the excitement and extra energy of the jockeys and horses right before or after a race. Later, he returned to his studio, where he modeled the horses in wax to help him see the animals from different angles. Sometimes, Edgar had a jockey pose on a dummy horse to recapture the exact moment from memory.

Edgar's art studio in Paris was in Montmartre, a lively and colorful part of the city. Taking Manet's advice, Edgar stopped making history paintings and started painting more portraits and scenes of everyday life.

"Painting isn't so difficult when you don't know how…But when you do…it's quite a different matter."

Edgar Degas

CAFÉ MON

Filled with artists, cafés, and nightclubs, the neighborhood had sweeping views of Paris and plenty of real people for Edgar to study. The young artist loved walking and exploring the city. He especially enjoyed spending hours arguing and discussing art with other artists and writers in the cafés.

Every year in Paris, the French Academy of Fine Arts (Académie des Beaux-Arts) selected pieces to be presented in the Salon, an exhibition that recognized the artwork of living artists. Artists competed to get their work into this very special exhibition. Manet encouraged Edgar to apply.

In 1867, Edgar submitted his painting *The Bellelli Family*. When he started the painting several years before he had always hoped it would make it into the Salon. Edgar was still adding the finishing touches until right before the painting was accepted to the show. When the exhibition opened, Edgar was excited to view his work— but the organizers had hung it in a place where people couldn't see it. Edgar was furious!

Edgar started using brighter colors and became even more interested in depicting movement and everyday life in Paris. Carrying his notebook everywhere, Edgar visited friends and family and sketched images of people doing simple things, like listening to music and doing laundry. He went to hat stores and restaurants, and started attending concerts and the theater to find new subjects to paint or draw.

When war broke out in 1870, Edgar and Manet joined the National Guard as volunteers to defend Paris. Even when the country was at war, Edgar continued to create art. He made sketches of his fellow soldiers in the French artillery. While he was training for rifle duty, Edgar learned that he had problems with his eyes, and he noticed that his sight had started to change.

After the war, Paris was unstable and there was political unrest and civil war. It wasn't a good time to be an artist in the city, so in 1872, when Edgar was 38 years old, he sailed to the United States to see his mother's family in New Orleans.

Edgar was captivated by the beauty and charm of the city. He was especially curious about his family's southern accents and even tried to learn how to imitate them!

Have you ever *visited* somewhere far away?

During his daily walks, Edgar would stroll by the colorful fruit markets, smell the orange and magnolia blossoms, and spy the billowing smoke from the steamboats. He loved New Orleans, but he missed Paris and was eager to go home.

When Edgar returned to France, he was no longer interested in showing his work at the Salon. He joined a group of other artists who felt the same way. The group would later be known as the Impressionists. The Impressionists, like Edgar, loved to capture moments in time in their paintings, like snapshots.

But many of the Impressionists preferred to paint outside, or *en plein air,* while Edgar preferred to paint in his studio.

Edgar was a leader in the group, but he often argued with the other artists, and considered himself a Realist painter, like Manet. Still, he helped to plan a show where he and his friends could show their work.

Sadly, before the exhibition, Edgar's father died. Then, Edgar discovered previously unknown family debt, and he was forced to sell the home and the art collection he inherited to pay back the money his father owed. For the first time in his life, Edgar had to rely on his artwork to survive.

In 1874, the first Impressionist exhibition took place. Edgar was represented with ten paintings, pastel drawings, and sketches. Edgar's work got good reviews, but compared to the Salon, the show was not popular. Few people attended and many who did thought it was a joke. They laughed at some of the artwork. Edgar's works were some of the few pieces that sold.

Edgar's favorite and most famous subjects were dancers at the Paris Opera, known in the city as "petits rats" (little rats). The young dancers were mostly girls from poor families. They worked tirelessly to become ballerinas to make a living.

Edgar liked showing the dancers in the middle of a performance, practicing in class, and at rest backstage. He caught every twist, turn, stretch, leap, and twirl on his sketch pad.

Like the dancers, Edgar repeatedly practiced. He wanted to get their movements and angles just right in his sketches. Sometimes the ballerinas caught Edgar humming along or tapping his toes to the music.

TAP

TAP

TAP

Edgar sketched the dancers in different poses to express the soft shapes of their graceful gestures. Then he went back to the studio to paint on canvas. There, he combined different drawings to create finished paintings.

Sometimes Edgar invented his own versions of the costumes, adding colorful ribbons, ruffles, sashes, and bows with pastels to make the dancers spring to life.

Dancing was one of the rare opportunities for women to work in Paris. Another was performing at the circus. At the Cirque Fernando, Edgar became fascinated by the strength and talent of the famous acrobat known as "Miss La La." Edgar drew her often, and most notably in his painting *Miss La La at the Cirque Fernando*. She is portrayed performing her most magnificent and thrilling stunt, which was being hoisted to the ceiling while holding on to a rope with just her teeth!

The Impressionists were one of the first art groups to include women. In 1877, Edgar invited American artist Mary Cassatt to show with the Impressionists, and they became close friends. Even though they grew up in different countries, the two artists had much in common. They both came from wealthy families, and neither had married or had children.

Cassatt appeared in several of Edgar's paintings, and they spent hours at each other's studios. Both loved to paint moments at the opera house and scenes from the daily lives of friends and strangers.

The artists learned from each other and grew. Sometimes they fought, and had heated discussions about art. They were both curious. They collaborated and explored techniques in printmaking, pastels, and metallic paint. Both artists collected each other's art, and their friendship lasted for over forty years!

Edgar always had an interest in experimenting with new materials. Around 1875, he started drawing with pastels.

While some other artists considered the use of pastels more suitable for children and amateurs, Edgar loved the vivid, juicy pigments. Unlike oil paint, which took time to dry, pastels were quick and easy to use. In his later works of art, when he was losing his eyesight, Edgar built up layers and layers of bright, luminous colors.

"Drawing is not what you see, but what you make others see."

Edgar Degas

When Edgar's eyesight weakened, it became easier for him to make sculptures than drawings.

His most famous sculpture, *Little Dancer of Fourteen Years*, started out as a sketch. Edgar built the base of the sculpture from old paintbrushes, metal, wood, and rope, then he covered it in wax. To make the dancer feel more real, Edgar added a little tulle skirt, dance slippers, a satin bow, and a horsehair wig.

Try forming a sculpture using foil or crumpled paper and tape!

When Edgar first exhibited the sculpture at the 1881 Impressionist exhibition, many people thought it was ugly and odd. It was the only sculpture he ever displayed in public. Years later, it is one of his most popular and celebrated creations!

Like many of his artist friends in France, Edgar was influenced by Japanese woodblock prints. Drawn to the bold colors, and the simple compositions of everyday life, Edgar and several of the Impressionists collected the prints.

Sketch someone doing something from everyday life, like washing dishes or doing homework!

Edgar liked that Japanese artists used unexpected angles. He used this technique to draw dancers, performers, and horses in motion.

In the mid-1880s, both Edgar and Cassatt were inspired by specific Japanese woodblock prints that featured themes of women bathing and brushing their hair. Edgar and Cassatt created their own versions of these works.

Why not have a **painting swap** with another arty friend?

When Edgar displayed a group of these pastels at the eighth and final Impressionist exhibition in 1886, critics were outraged by the strange poses of the models. After the show, Edgar gave one of the bathing pastels to Cassatt, and in exchange, she gave him her painting *Girl Arranging Her Hair.*

After eight art exhibitions between 1874 and 1886, the Impressionists decided to go their separate ways. The crowds had grown since their first show, and people were more interested in new styles of art. Many artists in the group, including Edgar, became successful. With Edgar's success, his financial situation improved, and he was able to start collecting art by his friends and other artists he admired. Edgar's work had also become famous and was displayed around the world.

By the 1890s, Edgar's eyesight was worse than ever before. He moved into a new studio, and started painting from memory. Edgar's years of practicing and perfecting his drawing skills allowed him to create beautiful works of art even when he could not see what he was creating.

On a trip to Burgundy, France, he made some landscape prints that were very popular. These works were shown in his first and only solo exhibition during his lifetime.

In the late 1880s, photography was a fairly new art form. Edgar picked up the camera to capture a moment in time. Sometimes he used his camera to set up models in poses that he would later sketch or paint, and sometimes he took portraits of friends and family at evening dinner parties.

Only about 50 of Edgar's photographs survive today.

In the early 1900s, Edgar used pastels more and more. The bright colors of the pastels were easier for him to see as his eyesight was fading. Edgar created a series of pastels of Russian dancers that were so thick and textured, they looked like they were sewn with thread. With big strokes and vivid pigments, these pictures glowed. Edgar continued to sell his work, but stepped back from public appearances.

As the years passed, Edgar slowed down and spent less time with his artist friends. In 1912, at the age of 78, he was forced from his home and studio in Montmartre, where he had lived and worked for over 20 years. The building was leveled to make room for a bigger structure. Edgar was upset that he was unable to make art, but he still spent his days exploring the city that he loved.

At the end of his life, Edgar surrounded himself with pictures he collected and created. He was one of France's leading artists, and he inspired younger painters, including Pablo Picasso and Henri Matisse.

When Edgar died in Paris at the age of 83, in 1917, he was recognized as a French national treasure.

"I don't want a funeral oration...you will say, 'He greatly loved drawing!'"

Edgar Degas

Edgar is celebrated as an artist who was a keen observer of everyday life. His ability to capture moving moments like snapshots in his compositions made his work unique and engaging.

Over his long career, Edgar dared to take chances, tested new methods, and inspired and learned from his fellow artists. He was able to show people how to see ordinary things in extraordinary new ways.

After Edgar's death, his family discovered 150 small wax and clay sculptures left behind in his studio. They had them cast in bronze and displayed the statues in museums and galleries around the world. Like his other works of art, they continue to dazzle viewers young and old to this day.

Timeline of key artworks

Over his career, Edgar experimented with different techniques. He used pastels, prints, paintings, photography, and sculpture to capture movements and moments. Here are a few of Edgar's key works, all in the collection of The Metropolitan Museum of Art.

1855–56
Self-Portrait
Oil on paper, laid down on canvas

1857–58
Young Woman with Ibis
reworked 1860-62
Oil on canvas

1865
A Woman Seated beside a Vase of Flowers
Oil on canvas

1867–68
James-Jacques-Joseph Tissot
Oil on canvas

"It is essential
to do the same
subject ten times,
a hundred times."

Edgar Degas

1873
A Woman Ironing
Oil on canvas

Timeline continued:

1874
The Rehearsal of the Ballet Onstage
Oil on canvas

1880
Little Dancer of Fourteen Years
Partially tinted bronze, cotton tarlatan, silk satin, and wood

1877
Dancers Practicing at the Barre
Mixed media on canvas

1884
The Singer in Greens
Pastel on light blue
laid paper

1882
At the Milliner's
Pastel on pale gray
wove paper, laid down
on silk bolting

1885-88
Race Horses
Pastel on wood

1892
Landscape
Monotype in oil colors,
heightened with pastel

Gesture Drawing

Edgar Degas often made art showing people in motion. Over his lifetime, he made more than 1,500 works portraying ballerinas dancing. Before he made a painting, Edgar would make several fast, flowing sketches of his subject in different poses. Gesture drawing is an exercise in which an artist makes quick, simple sketches of a subject, often a live model, to capture a movement or an action.

Edgar used black and white chalk to make this drawing of a young dancer. He added notes to the composition and several diagonal lines to show movement. He drew this same girl over and over again. Like the girl in the picture, Edgar was likely practicing several poses before making his final creation.

Try *this* yourself!

"Nothing in art must seem to be chance, not even a movement."

Edgar Degas

Little Girl Practicing at the Barre, **1878–80**
Black chalk and graphite, heightened with white chalk on pink laid paper.

First, find a sheet of paper, a pencil, and a friend to pose for you. Next, find a space where there is room to move.

Start by having your model try a few different poses to warm up. Make sure they have poses that extend their arms and legs to show action. They can pretend to be running, or stretching, or dancing.

Draw the curving, loose, flowing lines that follow the shape of the body. You can set a timer or have your friend count to 30 while you sketch. Have your model switch poses after each drawing. Make several sketches, then flip your paper over to use both sides.

Now it's your turn!

When you are done with a few drawings, switch with the model and have them be the artist! The goal of making gesture drawings is to study a subject and show how it moves.

Make a Sculpture!

The only sculpture Edgar Degas ever displayed in public was *Little Dancer of Fourteen Years*. The original sculpture was created from unusual materials, including old paintbrushes, metal, wood, and rope. Edgar covered the entire sculpture in wax, and then he added a real skirt, slippers, and a wig, tied with a ribbon.

After Edgar's death, his family found more than 150 wax and clay sculptures around his studio and had them cast in bronze. Much like his sketches, the sculptures were possibly used to practice his compositions. The human figures and horse sculptures he created show different variations of similar poses.

Challenge yourself!

Using clay, or objects from around the house, like paper, wire, and tape, create a sculpture that captures an interesting pose.

When you are done, use some fabric scraps or ribbon to add real details, like Edgar!

Glossary

Composition
The arrangement of elements in a painting or other work of art.

Critic
A person who judges the merits of a work of art.

En plein air (in the open air)
A manner of painting outdoors that became a central feature of French Impressionism.

Impressionists
A group of artists in the late 19th and early 20th centuries who paid special attention to light and its effect on subjects in their paintings.

Landscape
Art that depicts the natural environment.

Pastel
A crayon made of powdered pigments.

"Petits rats"
Name given to the young dancers at the Opera Ballet in Paris.

Portrait
A work of art created to show a person, animal, or group of people, usually focusing on the face.

Printmaking
An artistic process that involves transferring images onto another surface, most often paper or fabric.

Salon
An annual exhibition of the work of living artists held by the Royal Academy of Painting and Sculpture in Paris.

Amy Guglielmo

Amy Guglielmo is an author, educator, artist, and community arts and STEAM advocate. She has written many books for children, including *Cezanne's Parrot* and *Just Being Dali: The Story of Artist Salvador Dali*. Amy has co-authored the picture books *Pocket Full of Colors: The Magical World of Mary Blair*, winner of the Christopher Award; *How to Build a Hug: Temple Grandin* and *Her Amazing Squeeze Machine*; and the *Touch the Art* series of novelty board books featuring famous works of art with tactile additions. She lives in New York and Mexico with her husband.

Skylar White

Skylar White is a visual storyteller, currently living in New York City. She studied illustration at Rocky Mountain College of Art and Design in Denver, Colorado. When she is not painting, Skylar likes to go to a park or take walks around different parts of the city, always hoping to find a great vintage store. She takes inspiration from adventurous spirits, quiet moments, and everything in between. Her favorite stories to illustrate are ones that inspire young readers (and their adults!) to continue to learn and grow as we travel along.

Project Editor Rosie Peet
Project Art Editor Jon Hall
Art Director Clare Baggaley
Production Editor Siu Yin Chan
Production Controller Louise Minihane
Senior Acquisitions Editor Katy Flint
Managing Art Editor Vicky Short
Publishing Director Mark Searle

First American Edition, 2023
Published in the United States by DK Publishing
1745 Broadway, 20th Floor, New York, NY 10019

Page design copyright © 2023 Dorling Kindersley Limited
DK, a Division of Penguin Random House LLC
23 24 25 26 27 10 9 8 7 6 5 4 3 2 1
001–333561–May/2023

The Metropolitan
Museum of Art
New York

©The Metropolitan Museum of Art

All rights reserved.
Without limiting the rights under the copyright reserved above, no part of this
publication may be reproduced, stored in or introduced into a retrieval system,
or transmitted, in any form, or by any means (electronic, mechanical,
photocopying, recording, or otherwise), without the prior written
permission of the copyright owner.
Published in Great Britain by Dorling Kindersley Limited

A catalog record for this book
is available from the Library of Congress.
ISBN 978-0-7440-7070-5

DK books are available at special discounts when purchased
in bulk for sales promotions, premiums, fund-raising, or educational use.
For details, contact: DK Publishing Special Markets,
1745 Broadway, 20th Floor, New York, NY 10019
SpecialSales@dk.com

Printed and bound in Latvia

Acknowledgments
DK would like to thank Amy Charleroy, Laura Corey,
Rachel High, and Stephen Mannello at The Met; Martin Copeland and
Vagisha Pushp for picture research; Rica Dearman, Sophie Dryburgh and
Julia March for editorial assistance; Hilary Becker; Clare Baggaley;
Amy Guglielmo, and Skylar White.

The author would like to thank her dance teacher, Alice.

For the curious

www.dk.com
www.metmuseum.org

MIX
Paper | Supporting
responsible forestry
FSC™ C018179

This book was made with Forest
Stewardship Council™ certified
paper – one small step in DK's
commitment to a sustainable future.
**For more information go to
www.dk.com/our-green-pledge**

Sources for quotations
p. 11: National Gallery of Art, https://www.nga.gov/features/slideshows/edgar-degas.html
pp. 18, 30, 38, 41, 44: Edgar Degas, *Degas By Himself: Drawings, Prints, Paintings, Writings,* ed. Richard Kendall (New York: Barnes & Noble, 2004).

Picture credits
The publisher would like to thank The Metropolitan Museum of Art for their kind permission to reproduce works of art
from their collection and the following for additional permission to reproduce the copyrighted works of art:

(Key: a-above; b-below/bottom; c-center; f-far; l-left; r-right; t-top)

40-41 Shutterstock.com: Quirky Mundo (Background). **40 The Metropolitan
Museum of Art:** Bequest of Stephen C. Clark, 1960 (cla); Gift of Stephen Mazoh
and Purchase, Bequest of Gioconda King, by exchange, 2008 (cr); H. O. Havemeyer
Collection, Bequest of Mrs. H. O. Havemeyer, 1929 (bl). **41 The Metropolitan
Museum of Art:** H. O. Havemeyer Collection, Bequest of Mrs. H. O. Havemeyer,
1929 (br); Rogers Fund, 1939 (t). **42 The Metropolitan Museum of Art:** H. O.
Havemeyer Collection, Bequest of Mrs. H. O. Havemeyer, 1929 (tr, cla, bl). **42-43
Shutterstock.com:** Quirky Mundo (Background). **43 The Metropolitan Museum of
Art:** Bequest of Stephen C. Clark, 1960 (cra); H. O. Havemeyer Collection, Bequest
of Mrs. H. O. Havemeyer, 1929 (t); The Walter H. and Leonore Annenberg
Collection, Gift of Walter H. and Leonore Annenberg, 1999, Bequest of Walter H.
Annenberg, 2002 (bl); Purchase, Mr. and Mrs. Richard J. Bernhard Gift, 1972
(crb). **44 The Metropolitan Museum of Art:** H. O. Havemeyer Collection, Bequest
of Mrs. H. O. Havemeyer, 1929 (cr). **47 The Metropolitan Museum of Art:** H. O.
Havemeyer Collection, Bequest of Mrs. H. O. Havemeyer, 1929 (cr)
50 Ben Giebel: ca (Author's photo); **51 Skylar White:** tc.

All other images © Dorling Kindersley
For further information see: www.dkimages.com